The Pocket Epicurean

The Pocket Epicurean

John Sellars

THE UNIVERSITY OF CHICAGO PRESS

The University of Chicago Press, Chicago 60637
© 2021 by John Sellars
The author has asserted his moral rights.
Published 2021
Printed in the United States of America

30 29 28 27 26 25 24 23 22 21   1 2 3 4 5

ISBN-13: 978-0-226-79864-6 (cloth)
ISBN-13: 978-0-226-79878-3 (e-book)
DOI: https://doi.org/10.7208/chicago/9780226798783.001.0001

Originally published as *The Fourfold Remedy: Epicurus and the Art of Happiness* by Allen Lane, an imprint of Penguin Random House UK, 2021.

Library of Congress Cataloging-in-Publication Data

Names: Sellars, John, 1971– author.
Title: The pocket Epicurean / John Sellars.
Other titles: Fourfold remedy
Description: Chicago : The University of Chicago Press, 2021. |
    Includes bibliographical references.
Identifiers: LCCN 2021004320 | ISBN 9780226798646 (cloth) |
    ISBN 9780226798783 (ebook)
Subjects: LCSH: Epicureans (Greek philosophy)
Classification: LCC B512 .S45 2021 | DDC 187—dc23
LC record available at https://lccn.loc.gov/2021004320

♾ This paper meets the requirements of ANSI/NISO Z39.48-1992
(Permanence of Paper).

Contents

Prologue

WHAT DO WE really need in order to live a happy life? Many of us spend an inordinate amount of time and effort trying to secure the things that we *think we need* in order to live well. But how many of us have paused to think about what it is that we *actually need* in order to feel satisfied? Over two thousand years ago the Greek philosopher Epicurus did just that. He thought about what it is that we really desire and what we do and do not need in order to meet that desire. His answer was seemingly simple:

pleasure. All that we really want is pleasure. Today we tend to associate the word 'epicurean' with the enjoyment of fine food and wine, the gluttonous satisfaction of physical appetites, and decadent self-indulgence. But these things are a world away from the vision of a pleasant life developed by the original Epicureans. Epicurus was more concerned with mental pleasures than physical ones, and in some respects more concerned with avoiding pain than pursuing pleasure directly. His vision of the ideal human life focused not on satisfying one's physical appetites but rather on reaching a state free of all mental suffering. He called this *ataraxia*, literally 'untroubledness', but perhaps best translated as 'tranquillity'. That, he suggested, is what we are all really after, and he claimed to know how best to achieve it.

How might we overcome mental suffering and reach this state of tranquillity? Epicurus thought that first we need to identify the causes of our anxieties and then we need arguments to show us that those anxieties are groundless. We have no good reasons to worry about the things we do. Epicurus identified four sources of distress and proposed arguments designed to counter them. This led one of his later followers to call Epicurean philosophy 'the fourfold remedy'.

Over the centuries, Epicureanism has not always fared well. It has been associated with atheism, immorality, and gluttony of the senses. As a consequence it was for a long time demonized as a dangerous, corrupting doctrine. Nothing could be further from the truth. Epicurus advocated a modest life based on simple pleasures, all for the sake of attaining mental tranquillity here and now. The Epicurean message is that you already have everything you need, if only you could see it. Once you grasp that, all other anxieties will just melt away.

This book is, depending on your point of view, either a companion or a competitor to my *Pocket Stoic*. Epicurus was a contemporary of the founder of Stoicism, Zeno, and in antiquity the two schools were often presented as rival philosophies. Indeed, Epicureans and Stoics often argued against one another. While the Stoics advocated the cultivation of a virtuous character and saw Nature as rationally ordered, the Epicureans championed pleasure and thought the natural world was the chance product of chaos. Yet they also shared a lot of common ground. Both schools thought that all of our knowledge comes via our senses, that everything that exists is material, and that we die with our bodies. Both argued that a good life does not require a great deal of material possessions and both claimed that what matters most is attaining a tranquil state of mind. In antiquity the Stoic Seneca often quoted from both Epicurus and the Roman Epicurean poet Lucretius when he thought they had said something of universal value. In the early nineteenth century, Johann Wolfgang von Goethe commented that some people are temperamentally half Epicurean and half Stoic, upsetting the traditional view that these two schools of thought are fundamentally incompatible. More recently, Albert Ellis – founder of Rational Emotive Behaviour Therapy – listed Epicurus alongside the Stoics Epictetus and Marcus Aurelius as one of the ancient precursors of modern cognitive psychotherapy.

Epicureanism has much to teach us today. In an age rife with anxiety, it offers a path to peace of mind. In a culture of excessive material consumption, it prompts us to rethink how much we really need in order to live well. In an era of increasing social isolation, it reminds us of the value of friendship. Perhaps most importantly of all, when we are often surrounded by misinformation, it insists on the importance of unvarnished truth.

01

Philosophy as Therapy

'EMPTY ARE THE words of the philosopher who offers therapy for no human suffering.' So said the philosopher Epicurus, who was born and brought up on the Greek island of Samos towards the middle of the fourth century BC. He first became interested in philosophy as a teenager when, so the story goes, he was disappointed by his schoolteacher's inability to explain the central themes in Hesiod's poetry. His parents were originally from Athens and so Epicurus inherited their citizenship. When he turned eigh-

teen, Epicurus travelled to his family's native
city, perhaps to complete the military ser-
vice required of Athenian citizens. Around
the time that he was due to return home, his
family, along with other Athenian settlers,
were expelled from Samos, and Epicurus
found himself wandering from place to
place for a few years. For a while he lived in
Mytilene, on the island of Lesbos, where he
started to teach philosophy and met his life-
long friend Hermarchus. The locals did not
take kindly to his Athenian manner of pub-
lic philosophizing, so Epicurus, Hermarchus,
and perhaps a few others moved on to
Lampsacus on the mainland of Asia Minor,
in the general vicinity of ancient Troy. There,
over a number of years, Epicurus built up a
school of loyal followers, although this time
they kept themselves to themselves, having learned from the experience in Mytilene.
Eventually this community of kindred spirits
decided to move to Athens, where Epicurus
bought a patch of land just outside the city

walls. This became known as simply the Garden, and it was where Epicurus, his friends, and new admirers lived together in a simple life of self-sufficiency. The Garden flourished as a philosophical community for over two hundred years. It may have been brought to an end when the Garden was destroyed during an extended siege of the city by the Roman general Sulla in the early part of the first century BC, although Epicureans certainly continued to live in Athens afterwards.

Epicurus led his community of philosophers for some forty years. Together they shared a simple, communal life. Although other ancient philosophers had argued that friends ought to share property in common, the Epicurean Garden was no commune and each person retained their own private property. As we shall see later, this was important for Epicurus's own distinctive conception of friendship. When he died, Epicurus left both the Garden and his library of books to Hermarchus, his oldest friend, who took over as head of the community. Epicurus's birthday became a regular feast day and statues were erected in his honour. A cult of Epicurus developed, just as it did around the Buddha in India. Pliny the Elder reports that this continued among Roman admirers of Epicurus, who offered sacrifices on his birthday and carried around small portraits of him. This might make Epicureanism sound more like a religious movement than a philosophy based on dispassionate reason. Yet in the cases of both Epicurus and the Buddha, these were simply acts of admiration for mortal men preaching advice on how to overcome human suffering.

The devotion of Epicurus's followers could sometimes be extreme. Some five hundred years after Epicurus first came to Athens, an elderly admirer in a small town in Lycia (now south-western Turkey) erected a huge wall covered by a colonnade onto which he inscribed the philosopher's words for all to read. His name was Diogenes. The wall no longer stands but many of the blocks that once made it lie scattered around the ruins of the town – Oenoanda – and parts of the original inscription have been reconstructed. It's estimated that it was over forty metres long. Diogenes had carved into his wall his own accounts of Epicurean philosophy, along with sayings by Epicurus himself. Why did he do this? The expense must have been enormous. Fortunately Diogenes tells us himself near the beginning of the inscription: he did it in order to help his fellow citizens, whom he thought might benefit from some Epicurean therapy. Most people, he wrote, 'suffer from a common disease, with their false notions about things'. This confusion is endlessly spreading, Diogenes continued, for people infect each other like sick sheep. His inscription is intended to provide remedies; it is a medicine that brings salvation from false beliefs. Diogenes was confident that he had the right medicines, for he and other Epicureans had already put them to the test:

> We have dispelled the fears that grip us without justification, and, as for pains, those that are groundless we have completely excised, while those that are natural we have reduced to an absolute minimum.

Diogenes's accounts of Epicurean ideas were written in the form of letters, including one on physics and one on ethics. In this he was following Epicurus himself, who also wrote letters to friends summarizing the key ideas in his philosophy. There are three that survive: a letter to Herodotus (not the famous historian) outlining physical theory, a letter to Pythocles on meteorology, and a letter to Menoeceus concerned with ethics and, more broadly, how to live a good, happy life. These letters are among our most important sources for Epicurus's ideas.

In the opening lines of his *Letter to Menoeceus*, Epicurus presents his philosophy as something fundamentally therapeutic:

> No one should postpone the study of philos-
> ophy when he is young, nor should he weary
> of it when he becomes mature, because the
> search for mental health is never untimely or
> out of season.

The notion of mental health – literally
'hygiene of the soul' – is thus nothing new.
Philosophy is of perennial importance, Epicurus continued, because it is the one thing
that can help us attain happiness, which, he
added, is the one thing that we are all after:
'when we have this we have everything, and
we do everything we can to get it when we
don't have it'.

Can philosophy deliver happiness? For
Epicurus the key is to attain a calm, tranquil mind. How do we get there? We do so
by overcoming the twin perils of frustrated
desires and anxiety about the future, and
Epicurus thought that his philosophy had
powerful remedies for these two causes of

psychological disquiet. It is by taking on board his arguments about these things that, he claimed, we can achieve the happiness we all desire.

In this sense Epicurus's philosophy is indeed a form of psychological therapy. As we noted earlier, Albert Ellis saw Epicureanism as a type of cognitive psychotherapy, standing alongside Stoicism and Buddhism in holding that our emotional disturbances are primarily a product of how we see the world and as such something that we can control. But if that's the case, why did Epicurus also write letters dealing with physics and meteorology? What do these subjects have to do with mental health? The answer is simple: many of our fears and anxieties are the result of failing to see things as they really are, whether that's not truly understanding what we need in order to flourish or imagining threats that don't really exist. It is knowledge of how the world works that will set us free, Epicurus insisted.

This idea that the study of physics ought to play a central part in the cure of mental disturbances is at the heart of the work of Epicurus's most famous follower, Lucretius. We don't know much about Lucretius's life except that he was a Roman who lived in the first century BC, possibly in the Bay of Naples area, where he may have been part of a larger Epicurean community. His only surviving work is a poem, *On the Nature of Things*, dedicated to the goddess Venus, which is mostly devoted to explaining and defending Epicurean physical theory. It is addressed to Memmius, probably the Roman politician Gaius Memmius, who was perhaps Lucretius's patron, and who at one point owned the ruins of Epicurus's house in Athens.

Lucretius's poem is primarily concerned with giving naturalistic – and more specifically atomistic – explanations of everything, from the formation of the universe to the development of human technology (we'll come back to atomism later). Yet one of its striking features is that Lucretius regularly reminds his readers that his primary motivation for trying to understand the natural world is the therapeutic benefit that such understanding can bring.

The great enemy throughout *On the Nature of Things* is superstition – false and confused beliefs that cause people to behave in all sorts of unhelpful ways. Towards the beginning of the first book Lucretius writes:

> This dread and darkness of the mind cannot be dispelled by the sunbeams, the shifting shafts of day, but only by an understanding of the outward form and inner workings of nature.

That Lucretius thought these lines were important is underlined by the fact that he repeats them word for word three more times later on in the poem. It is only reason that can cure us of the anxieties and fears that keep us awake at night, he insists elsewhere. The way reason can do this is

by uncovering the true 'nature of things'.
His presentation of this rational, scientific
medicine in verse is analogous, he tells us,
to the doctor who sugar-coats his pills. The
ability of philosophy to transform our lives in
this way led Lucretius to hail it as the great-
est human creation – more important even
than the invention of farming! – because it
is impossible to live a happy, tranquil life
without it.

Lucretius was not the only Epicurean
in Rome and, as noted, he may have been
part of a community of Epicureans located
around the Bay of Naples. One of the leading figures in this group was the Epicurean
teacher Siro, who counted the poet Virgil
among his students. Indeed, after Siro's
death, Virgil inherited his house. In one of
Virgil's early poems, we find sentiments very
close to those we've just seen in Lucretius:

> Happy is he who can know the causes of
> things

> And crush under foot all fear
> Of unyielding fate and ravenous hell.

Another famous Roman poet influenced by Epicurean ideas was Horace. This comes through most clearly in his *Satires*. Both Virgil and Horace were influenced by Philodemus, a poet and Epicurean philosopher also based in the Bay of Naples, whom we shall meet properly later. Beyond these literary figures, Epicureanism also found admirers among the political figures in Rome, including Brutus and Cassius, now remembered for their part in the assassination of Julius Caesar. On the other side of that particular dispute, Caesar's own father-in-law, Lucius Calpurnius Piso, also seems to have had Epicurean sympathies. He owned a villa in the town of Herculaneum on the Bay of Naples, not far from Pompeii, which may have been a focal point for the local Epicurean community. Piso was probably the patron of a number of Epicureans, the most important of whom was Philodemus, and the library at Piso's villa contained a wide variety of Epicurean works, including many by Philodemus and some by Epicurus himself.

It was in this idyllic environment on the Italian coast, away from the daily intrigues of Rome, that Epicureans such as Lucretius, Virgil, Philodemus, and others tried to recreate the spirit of Epicurus's Garden. They embraced the key Epicurean ideas that philosophy is therapy and that salvation comes through understanding how the world works.

02

The Path to Tranquillity

IN MODERN ENGLISH the word 'epicurean' has come to mean someone who delights in physical pleasures such as fine food and wine. The image of the Epicurean as a greedy pig, though, is not new. Even in antiquity it was common to associate Epicureanism with pigs. In a letter to one of his friends, the poet Horace jokingly described himself as 'fat and flourishing, a hog from Epicurus's herd'. One ancient critic spread the rumour that Epicurus vomited twice a day due to overeating. Another suggested that the philosopher and his followers consorted with prostitutes. Stoics accused him of effeminacy. In reality, Epicurus lived an extremely modest life, content with bread and water, supplemented with some cheese as an occasional luxury.

So how did this reputation come about? It was because Epicurus claimed that pleasure is the key to a good life. Pleasure is good and pain is bad, so pursue pleasure and avoid pain. Epicurus thought that this is both the origin and the goal of all we do. It's the origin in the sense that we instinctively pursue pleasure and avoid pain, and it's the goal in the sense of being what all our actions are ultimately trying to achieve. The problem is that all too often we overcomplicate things for ourselves. In fact, life is very simple: pursue pleasure and avoid pain. That's it.

That makes it sound incredibly simple, perhaps too much so. Epicurus's view was in fact far more nuanced and sophisticated than that. He drew a number of distinctions between different kinds of pleasure. One

of the most important was between what
he called active and static pleasures. We
might think of this as the difference between
pleasure gained from a process or an action
and the pleasure of being in a certain state or
condition – doing versus being. For instance,
we might distinguish between the active
pleasure of eating and the subsequent static
pleasure of being full up and no longer hungry. Although we might enjoy the process of
eating, Epicurus argued that the reason *why*
we eat is in order to reach the state of not
being hungry. Our goal is not the pleasure of
eating, but overcoming the pain of hunger.
In this sense, Epicureanism is quite different
from the image of the modern 'epicure' who
revels in fine dining. The goal is pleasure, but
it is not more and more active pleasure; it is
reaching a state of static pleasure, of contentment. It's not the pleasure of eating, it's the
contentment of not being hungry. And for
Epicurus, not being hungry is not merely the
absence of pain, which sounds like a fairly

bland, neutral state; it is itself an instance
of pleasure. This is because he thought that
there is no neutral state between pleasure
and pain. We are never in a completely
unfeeling state. The absence of pain is itself a
pleasurable state to be in, while a life devoid
of all pleasure would be painful to endure.

There's one further important point to
make about this. Active pleasures can vary
in quantity – you can always eat more and
more. But the state of contentment you reach
when you are full and no longer hungry
cannot vary at all. Once you are full, you are
full, and if you keep eating you won't become
even more 'not hungry'. You won't add any
further static pleasure. Indeed, you'll probably end up with indigestion, generating pain
rather than more pleasure. So there's a clear
limit to the pursuit of pleasure, Epicurus
thought. The limit is reached when one
reaches this state of static pleasure. As Epicurus put it, 'bodily pleasure is not enlarged
once the pains brought on by need have been

done away with; it is only diversified.' In other words, once we are no longer hungry, further food just gives us variation, which is superficial compared to the basic need to overcome the pain of hunger. The pursuit of pleasure turns out in fact to be the pursuit of not being in pain – not being hungry, cold, ill, or any other condition that we would rather avoid. Epicurean pleasure, then, has nothing to do with gluttony. It's a modest affair aimed at a state of contentment that does not require much at all.

So far we've just been talking about physical pleasures and pains: the active pleasure of eating and the static pleasure of not being hungry. Although Epicurus did think that these basic physical pleasures were ultimately the foundation of everything else, he was in fact far more preoccupied with what goes on in our minds. Although the physical pain of being hungry is never a nice thing to experience, it can be endured without too much discomfort, at least for a while.

But mental suffering such as fear or anxiety can be far more debilitating and can colour a person's whole life. Consequently, these became Epicurus's main concerns.

One of the reasons for Epicurus's focus on mental pleasures and pains came out of reflection about what really troubles us. The person fearful of going to the dentist suffers far more distress from the anxiety *about* going than they do from the drill when they are anaesthetized in the chair. Many of us spend significant mental energy worrying about not having enough money in the future while in fact having everything that we need right now. At the same time, real physical pain – the stubbed toe or the aching back – is unpleasant for a short time but usually soon forgotten. We are actually quite good at coping with physical pain, yet we still manage to generate huge amounts of mental pain worrying about physical suffering that may or may not happen in the future. The bulk of our suffering, then, is internal and

self-inflicted. But at least that means it's
something we have the power to fix.

At the same time, physical pleasures are
fast and fleeting. The good meal is forgotten
a day later. But the mental pleasure derived
from good conversation with friends over
that same meal is something more likely to
stick with us. Indeed, reflecting back on that
conversation can generate further mental
pleasure for us here and now. In the cases of
both pain and pleasure, then, it's the mental
ones that matter most to the quality of our
lives.

We now have four different types of pleasure according to Epicurus: active physical
pleasures such as eating, static physical
pleasure such as not being hungry, active
mental pleasures such as enjoying conversation with friends, and static mental pleasures
such not being disturbed by anything. All of
these are inherently good things, he claimed,
but the most important by far is the last one:
static mental pleasure – not being anxious,

worried, or afraid. This is, in effect, the psychological equivalent of not being hungry. The word that Epicurus used to describe this state was *ataraxia*, literally 'not being troubled', but usually translated as 'tranquillity'.

It's tranquillity that we really want, the absence of mental disturbance. We'd also like to avoid physical pain if we can. For an Epicurean this too is an inherently bad thing. But Epicurus thought that physical suffering is much easier to endure. One way in which we can come to cope with it is by counterbalancing it with mental pleasures. A long day on holiday, for instance, visiting new and interesting places, may leave you with sore feet and a pounding headache. But these are easily offset by the mental stimulation of the day and we'll look back on the trip overall as a positive and pleasant experience.

In a sense, then, an Epicurean is engaged in weighing up different pleasures and pains in order to see what the overall picture looks like. This sort of process is sometimes referred to as 'hedonistic calculus'. Epicurus suggested that often we might choose to forego an immediate pleasure or put up with pain without complaint, because we know that in the long run it will be worth it. We'll avoid some immediate pleasures if we think they might produce pains later on. 'No pleasure is bad in itself,' he commented, 'but the things that make for pleasure in certain cases entail disturbances many times greater than the pleasures themselves.' Equally we'll put up with immediate pain if we think it will result in greater pleasure later on, or even just enable us to avoid larger pains further down the line. Consequently, although every pleasure is something good, that doesn't mean that every pleasure is worth pursuing. It will come down to a reflective process of judgement and calculation. But the key point is that Epicurus thought mental pleasures will always outweigh physical pains, and so it's the inner working of our mental lives that ought to be the main focus of our attention, not the superficial physical pleasures that people associate with hedonism today. Even a memory of a past pleasure can outweigh an immediate, intense physical pain, Epicurus claimed. As Horace put it in one of his Epicurean moments, 'the highest pleasure resides not in an expensive aroma but in yourself'. Unsurprisingly, scented candles turn out not to be the answer.

Epicurus also offered other thoughts to try to help people cope with physical suffering. Pain usually falls into two categories, he suggested: if it is intense, it is usually short lived, while if it is lingering it is usually mild. In either case the knowledge that it will be *either* short lived *or* mild can help to reduce the mental anxiety that often accompanies pain, such as worry about our ability to cope with it. On those rare occasions where intense pain does go on for a while, it – or whatever is causing it – will probably kill us, bringing it to an end anyway. That might not sound like much consolation, but the important Epicurean point is that we ought not to be fearful about physical pain. We can learn to cope with it and we are unlikely to have to suffer extreme pain for any great length of time. On its own terms it is manageable and when placed on the scales next to mental pleasures it soon falls into the background.

Unlike the caricature of a hedonist lifestyle, then, Epicureanism proposes a far more complex and sophisticated image of a life devoted to pleasure. In his *Letter to Menoeceus*, Epicurus wrote that a pleasant life is not one devoted to drinking parties, fine food, or carnal desires:

> On the contrary, it is the result of sober thinking – namely investigation of the reasons for every act of choice and aversion and elimination of those false ideas about the gods and death which are the chief source of mental disturbance.

We'll come back to the gods and death later on. Before we get to them we'll consider our choices and aversions, or, to put it in other words, what we think we need in order to live a good life. But already we can see that whatever external things may or may not be required, reflective philosophical thinking is the non-negotiable foundation. Epicurus had no doubts about how powerful and trans-formative this could be. He concluded his letter to his friend Menoeceus by stressing its importance:

> Think about these and related matters day and night, by yourself and in company with someone like yourself. If you do, you will never experience anxiety, waking or sleeping, but you will live like a god among men.

03

What Do You Need?

WHAT DO YOU need in order to live a pleasant life? A place of your own, a nice car, a good job to pay for these things? What we think we need might vary a lot depending on who we are, to whom we compare ourselves, and the expectations of the society in which we live. A few years ago a news story in a national newspaper in Great Britain recounted the woes of a middle-class couple in London who were struggling to get by on an income of £150,000 a year (some five times the national average). Unsurprisingly, they received little sympathy from those readers who could only dream of earning that kind of money. What we think we need looks to be highly subjective and relative to our particular situation.

These sorts of issues are nothing new. In the first century BC, Horace reflected on the same concerns in Rome. No one, he commented, seems happy with what they've got. People continually desire more and more, regarding with envy those who have more than them:

> 'Nothing is enough,' they say, 'for you're only worth what you have.' What can you do with a man like that? You may as well tell him to be miserable, since misery is what he enjoys.

Imagine being in a continual state of misery produced by greed and envy; that's no way to live. If we do manage to amass enough in the way of money and material possessions to overcome such feelings, then, Horace comments, we will be overtaken by new anxieties:

Maybe you prefer to lie awake half dead with fright, to spend your days and nights in dread of burglars or fire or your own slaves, who may fleece you and then disappear?

If those are the blessings of material success, Horace adds, then perhaps poverty is not so bad after all. It's the endless race for wealth that's the problem: the constant feeling that, no matter how much we have, it will never be enough. How much do we have to have in order to escape the fear of not having enough?

Epicurus's approach to this question was to strip things back down to basics. What do we actually *need*? What is essential for our physical survival? Food, water, shelter from the elements; that's about it. These are nature's demands. Epicurus called the desire for these sorts of things 'natural and necessary'. But what if you want not just shelter but your own private shelter, in a nice part of town, perhaps with a fancy new kitchen?

And what if you want not merely food, but interesting, well-presented food, along with a decent glass of wine? That's all fine, Epicurus would say, and perfectly reasonable. The desire for these sorts of things clearly grows out of our more basic natural desires for food, water, and shelter, even if it goes beyond what is absolutely essential. Epicurus called these sorts of things 'natural, but not necessary'. They are nice to have but you can, and indeed millions of people do, live perfectly happily without them.

Then there's everything else: all the other things that we presumably think we need in order to live a happy life, given how much money some people are prepared to spend on them: the latest technological gadgets, jewellery and fancy watches, and so on. For Epicurus these sorts of things would fall into his third category of things, the 'unnatural and unnecessary'. Not only do we not need them, they don't even serve a useful natural purpose.

So, what do you need? For Epicurus, the answer is clear. The only things you need are those that are natural and necessary. The rest is mere window dressing. What you *need* is actually very little and, because of that, is fairly easy to secure. 'Nature's wealth,' Epicurus wrote, 'is restricted and easily won, while that of empty convention runs on to infinity.' While it is a tragedy that some people in the developed world still struggle to afford the basics of life, not to mention the struggles to survive endured by people elsewhere in the world, many of us are fortunate enough not to have to face the real possibility of ever having to go without food altogether. We are instead absorbed in trying to secure all the other stuff that Epicurus insisted is unnecessary. That doesn't mean that we shouldn't ever pursue all the window dressing. But Epicurus would want to make two points. The first is that it would be crazy to get overly upset about not managing to secure things that we don't actually need, especially if the ultimate goal is to enjoy a pleasant, tranquil life that would be compromised by getting upset. The second is that *knowing* that what we really need is actually very little, and so fairly easy to get, will remove much of the anxiety we have about getting what we think we need. That knowledge will itself contribute to our mental tranquillity. Suddenly the pressure is off. 'One who understands the limits of the good life,' Epicurus wrote, 'knows that what eliminates the pains brought on by need and what makes the whole of life perfect is easily obtained, so that there is no need for enterprises that entail the struggle for success.'

In this sense Epicurus wanted to set a limit to our desires, just as he set a limit on the pursuit of pleasure. In both cases it's possible to work out what's enough. We don't need to get caught on what is sometimes called 'the hedonic treadmill', constantly pursuing more things for the sake of more pleasure. As Epicurus himself put it, 'nothing

is sufficient for the person who finds suffi-
ciency too little'. There is in fact a clear limit
to what we need: enough food in order not to
be hungry, enough warmth and shelter not
to be cold, and so on. Not only that, *knowing*
that our physical needs are fairly easily met
will itself take care of a good number of our
psychological worries. Knowledge derived
from philosophical reflection is the key to
mental equanimity.

One of the problems, though, is that it's so
easy to get caught up in all those natural but
unnecessary desires. Many of us are fortunate enough to be able to enjoy these sorts of
things much of the time. How often do you
have to rely on just bread and water in order
to survive? The problem is that once we've
become accustomed to enjoying a varied and
interesting diet, we all too easily complain in
situations when it's not available. We come to
see these things as necessary for our happiness, when in fact they're not. It was not that
long ago when almost no one bought a cup of

coffee during their morning commute; now many people seem to see it as a more or less essential part of their routine. Technological gadgets and services that only a decade or so ago didn't even exist increasingly feel like necessary bits of everyday life. Part of this is simply the product of familiarity and habit; we become used to these new things surprisingly quickly. There are also, of course, companies that are very keen to make us feel that their new products are 'must have' additions to our lives. And once they are a part of our lives they soon become integrated to the point that their absence seems like a real deprivation.

How do we get round this? One option would be to avoid such things altogether, adopting a far more ascetic way of life. That would be one way of escaping the trap. Although some people have seen Epicurus as a fairly ascetic figure, proposing that we avoid unnecessary things completely, I don't think that's quite what he's suggesting.

There's nothing at all wrong with enjoying the very best of culinary pleasures when they present themselves, so long as we don't come to expect them at every meal. Fine dining may not be required for us to satisfy our hunger, but it does offer welcome variety. The way to avoid coming to expect this all the time, Epicurus suggested, is to be suitably grateful whenever we are fortunate enough to be able to enjoy such pleasures. One way to develop a suitably appreciative attitude may well involve not overindulging, even when we have the opportunity to do so. It turns out, then, that in fact some mild asceticism might be in order. This is not to suggest that we should deny ourselves pleasures all the time. Instead it would encourage us to moderate our consumption so that we properly appreciate unnecessary pleasures when we do indulge. The problem is not with enjoying; it is with taking things for granted. Epicurus himself once wrote to a friend saying that bread and water were more than enough for most occasions, but a small pot of cheese made a nice treat once in a while.

Epicurus also thought that adopting this attitude towards our desires will make us more generous. The wise person who has recalibrated his desires in line with what is strictly necessary will, Epicurus wrote, 'understand better how to share than to take – so large is the fund of self-sufficiency that they have discovered'. If we can see that we don't need much, then when we have more than we strictly need, we'll be happy to share with those around us, strengthening our bonds of friendship in the process.

Not only that, knowing that we don't need very much will also secure our freedom and autonomy, for if we can see that we don't need very much, then we won't be beholden to anyone else. Epicurus put it like this:

> A free person cannot acquire many possessions, because this is no easy feat without becoming a hireling of mobs or dynasts. And yet

they have a constant abundance of everything, and if they should chance to gain many possessions, they could easily portion them out so as to win their neighbours' goodwill.

It's the self-sufficiency of a simple life, then, that secures our freedom. As we saw earlier, Horace reflected on the ways in which possessions can create anxiety about their loss, reducing us to a state of fear. All these things amassed supposedly in order to help us avoid physical pain simply end up generating mental suffering instead and, as we have seen, Epicurus was insistent that that's a far more pernicious form of distress. If we want to escape this anxiety, if we want to avoid slavery to empty desires, then we need to learn that what we *really* need is in fact very little and in most circumstances can be obtained quite easily.

04

The Pleasures
of Friendship

LIFE ISN'T SIMPLY a matter of satisfying our physical needs. Most of us know this already. What matters most to the vast majority of people are their relationships with others, whether that be with friends, family, or partners. It's often other people who are central to our image of what a happy life will look like.

From the beginning Epicurus lived his philosophy with others. He set up his Garden community in Athens with his friends as an experiment in communal living. Many of those friends came with him from Lampsacus and Mytilene, and his three brothers also joined the community. Although he argued that we don't need much stuff in order to enjoy a happy life, Epicurus appears to have taken the role played by other people very seriously. Indeed, he developed a fascinating account of friendship that not only explains its sometimes fragile nature, but also why it is so important to us.

To begin, we might reflect on what we think a friend is, and what distinguishes a friend from a mere acquaintance or a stranger. According to Epicurus one of the defining characteristics of a true friend is that you can rely on them in times of need. Conversely, if you are a true friend then others will be able to rely on you. Friends care about each other in a way that passing acquaintances usually don't.

So, a friend is someone we can rely on when we need help. We hope that we won't need to depend on them too often, but at least we know they are there. Indeed, Epicurus thought that this was just as important, if not more so, than direct practical help. It's *knowing* that we have people to whom we can turn in a crisis that's the key, even if we rarely or never actually call on their assistance. As Epicurus himself put it, what matters is not so much direct help as confidence that such help is at hand should we ever need it. Knowing that this kind of support is out there and available can significantly reduce our anxiety about the future, he thought.

Having said all that, someone who treats their friends as *merely* a support network is probably not much of a friend at all. For a start, the support must go both ways: we must be as willing to give support at a moment's notice as we would be relieved to receive support when we need it most. Then, there's a question of balance. Someone who continually asks for or expects help might be seen to be overstepping the mark of what's reasonable to assume from a friend. Their excessive demands might also make a relationship one-sided. At the other extreme, a friend who never asks for or accepts help might seem too disconnected. Not only that, one might feel awkward turning to them for help in a crisis, if they've never accepted any themselves. So, there needs to be a reciprocal flow of support both ways. Just how much support will no doubt depend on the friendship, so long as both parties feel that they are getting as much out of it as they are putting in. Some friendships involve a constant flow back and forth of practical and moral support; others might be a bit more reserved. Yet according to Epicurus, in order to count as a proper friendship there will always be that unspoken knowledge that if things take a turn for the worse there's someone you know you can rely on. The best type of friend, Epicurus commented, doesn't reduce a relationship to mutual support but neither do they deny the role that such support plays.

As he put it, the former reduces friendship to a mere commercial transaction, while the latter destroys any sense of security for the future.

All this might help to explain why friendship can sometimes be a fragile affair. It's a complex balancing act based on a number of usually unspoken assumptions. We may not explicitly say to our friends that we'll be there to support them in a time of crisis, and we are even less likely to ask them to confirm that they'll be there to support us. This all goes unsaid. True friends don't keep a tally of how often one person has helped the other – that would indeed reduce it to little more than a commercial transaction – but at the same time if the flow of support only goes one way, the friendship may become lopsided and struggle to last. There will no doubt be exceptional cases where these principles don't neatly apply, but in general Epicurus's reflections on friendship seem to capture something important. It's a relationship of mutual care and support that avoids collapsing into a mere exchange of favours.

Beyond that practical support, friendship can also involve what we might call moral support, in the form of sympathy and toleration. When reflecting on the role of friendship, Horace suggested that friends are much more likely to be generous when describing each other's faults: the tight-fisted friend is described as 'careful with money', while the show-off is called 'amusing company'. We tolerate our friends' foibles and mistakes, and hope that they will do the same for us. 'My kind friends will forgive me if, as a result of being a fool, I do something wrong,' Horace wrote, adding, 'I in turn will gladly overlook their lapses.'

Why was friendship so important to Epicurus? I think there are two reasons why he paid it careful attention. The first is the idea that knowing we have people we can turn to in times of difficulty, even if we never need to, can help to reduce anxiety about the future. Removing that anxiety directly contributes to the goal of Epicurus's philosophy: reaching a state of mental tranquillity. The second reason involves a detour into his wider thinking about politics.

Epicurus was fairly distrustful of conventional politics. He did not get involved in the politics of Athens and he counselled his followers to 'live unnoticed' rather than get embroiled in such matters themselves. He was also sceptical about the foundations on which political communities claimed to be based. In many cases this was, implicitly at least, a version of what nowadays people call 'social contract theory'. This is the idea that people willingly submit to the system of justice created by a political community in order to benefit from the protection it offers. The state of nature, as Thomas Hobbes put it almost two thousand years later, is a war of all against all, so people come together to form communities, trading some of their freedoms in exchange for mutual safety. This,

according to Epicurus, is how the notion
of justice came about. It is the product of
a contract between people concerned with
not harming others and not being harmed
oneself. A political community arranged
according to a system of justice like this is
ultimately grounded on feelings of suspicion and fear – suspicion about the motives
of other people and fear of being harmed
if the justice system were not there to curb
their behaviour. Once that system is in place,
people are expected to follow the rules of the
community, again out of a sense of fear – fear
of being caught and punished if they break
the rules. This can hardly be a healthy foundation for a community, Epicurus thought.
By contrast, a community of people based on
the Epicurean idea of friendship would be
one grounded in mutual care and support,
with unspoken assurances of help rather
than formal rules and regulations. This,
then, is a second reason why Epicurus placed
so much weight on friendship: it offers a

quite different and more positive model for what a community of people might look like, and presumably it was the model for his own community in the Garden.

It is difficult to know for sure just what the Garden community was like. We know that it welcomed both men and women, leading to all sorts of gossip among Athenians who didn't know what was going on behind the Garden's walls. Despite living communally, it has often been presumed that members retained their own private property. Epicurus himself also possessed a house of his own within the city walls of Athens that was presumably his private residence. His account of friendship has been taken to presuppose that individuals retained some private means. Although there are, of course, all sorts of ways in which friends can help each other out that don't require private financial resources, it looks as if Epicurus's vision presupposes that kind of assistance too. After all, how can having friends reduce your anxiety about falling into extreme poverty if they don't themselves have the resources necessary to help you out in an emergency? Either way, the important lesson for us is that our friendships can play a vital role in both our material and psychological well-being.

So far we've focused on the practical and material benefits that can come from friends. But there's another, far more straightforward, way in which we gain something important from such relationships. What we gain is the simple pleasure of spending time with people whose company we enjoy. As we all know, this can take many forms, from animated conversation over dinner to silently watching television together, and from intimate romantic encounters to mass gatherings of like-minded people at festivals, sporting events, and the like. This kind of psychological pleasure is valuable for its own sake, is often far more satisfying than the physical pleasures of crude hedonism, and, best of all, it's free. Knowing that some of the very best pleasures that life can offer are readily available without cost from our friends can only add to our sense of self-sufficiency and freedom. All of the benefits that come from friendship provoked Epicurus to break from his usually sober turn of phrase when in a moment of exuberance he wrote, 'Friendship dances around the world, summoning every one of us to awaken to blessedness.' Of all the things that contribute to our happiness, Epicurus insisted that friendship is the most important.

05

Why Study
Nature?

IF PHILOSOPHY IS primarily concerned with our mental health, why did Epicurus place so much emphasis on the study of nature? Epicurus didn't merely dip into theoretical studies of the natural world, he wrote about it at great length. His magnum opus, *On Nature*, extended to thirty-seven books. This huge work was completely lost until, in the mid-eighteenth century, a remarkable discovery was made in the shadow of Mount Vesuvius. The towns of Pompeii and

Herculaneum were buried after the famous eruption of 79 AD. At Herculaneum excavations by tunnel discovered the remains of a large villa containing many treasures, not least a vast library of papyrus scrolls. The villa, now known as the Villa of the Papyri, was probably once the home of Lucius Calpurnius Piso, the father-in-law of Julius Caesar.

While there was great hope that these charred papyrus scrolls, resembling lumps of coal, might contain within them lost masterpieces of classical literature, there was some disappointment when it turned out that many of the texts that could be deciphered were merely works of Epicurean philosophy. Even so, the importance of the finds could not be underestimated. What early scholars found were a number of books from Epicurus's previously lost *On Nature* along with a whole series of works by an Epicurean called Philodemus.

Philodemus was originally from Gadara,

in modern-day Jordan, not far from the Sea
of Galilee. He was born sometime around
110 BC. After spending his childhood in
Gadara, Philodemus left home probably in
the pursuit of an education, heading first to
Alexandria, and then on to Athens. There
he studied with Zeno of Sidon, who was
then head of the Epicurean Garden. For
reasons that are not entirely clear, Philodemus left Athens – perhaps around the time
of the Roman siege of the city that led to
the destruction of the Garden – and headed
to Italy, settling in the Bay of Naples area,
possibly after a short period in Rome. He
probably brought copies of Epicurean texts
with him from Athens, and it has been suggested that one of the copies of Epicurus's *On
Nature* discovered in the Villa of the Papyri
originally belonged to Philodemus's teacher
Zeno. Philodemus appears to have lived by
the Italian coast for the rest of his life. For
centuries he was remembered as the writer
of short epigrams, but the discoveries at

Herculaneum secured his reputation as an important Epicurean philosopher.

The task of recovering these Epicurean texts from the charred papyrus scrolls has been laborious to say the least. The first excavators didn't even recognize them as scrolls and who knows what texts were lost as some were simply thrown onto fires. Others were so brittle that they crumbled into pieces on touch. The first attempts to open them more or less all ended in the destruction of the scroll. Some progress was made after the King of Naples sought assistance from the Vatican Library, who sent Antonio Piaggio to oversee proceedings; the first recovered texts were published in 1793. An English clergyman sent by the Prince Regent, John Hayter, managed to open some 200 scrolls, transcribing what could be read before the blackened papyrus crumbled away. Some of Hayter's drawings were sent back to England and are now the only witness we have for the ancient texts he managed briefly to glimpse.

One such text, which survives only thanks to a faint nineteenth-century pencil drawing, now in a library in Oxford, is a short summary of the essence of Epicurean philosophy composed by Philodemus. It is known as the *tetrapharmakos* – the fourfold remedy – and it goes like this:

> Don't fear God,
> Don't worry about death.
> What's good is easy to get,
> What's terrible is easy to endure.

The four lines capture key Epicurean ideas about God, death, pleasure, and pain, summarizing the contents of the first four of Epicurus's *Key Doctrines*. We've already touched on the ideas in the second half of these four lines, but what about the first half? 'Don't fear God, / Don't worry about death.' For the Epicureans, fear of God and concern about death were two of the most common forms of anxiety, and the two most urgently requiring treatment. We'll consider Epicurean reflections about death in the next chapter. Here let's focus on fear of God.

Epicurus's response to this kind of fear began, perhaps unexpectedly, with the study of meteorology. Epicurus wrote an entire letter about the subject to his friend Pythocles. It was evidently a topic that he thought to be especially important, precisely because he believed it would help to promote a happy life. No other end is served by the study of such things, he wrote, than the cultivation of tranquillity. If we want that, we need to see how things really are, rather than falling back on mere assumptions or prejudices.

Everything that there is, Epicurus argued, is made of atoms, which exist in an infinite void. These atoms come together to form larger aggregates through random collisions. This is how our planet and other celestial bodies came to be formed. The more we can understand the processes through which these things came about, the less likely we shall be to attribute them to the action of some unknown and imaginary deity. And Epicurus insisted that the information people already had from observations provided plenty of evidence for his view. This is something we must accept because, he wrote, 'if a person fights the clear evidence of his senses he will never be able to share in genuine tranquillity'. Strictly speaking, Epicurus would have to say that he had no direct sensory evidence for the existence of atoms, but he would argue that atomic theory offered by far the best explanation for the things that we do experience via the senses, and that's why we should embrace it.

Having considered the formation of celestial bodies, Epicurus turned to topics that fall under what we now think of as meteorology – thunder, lightning, hail, snow, and the like. Thunder, he suggested, may be caused by wind rolling around inside clouds, although he considers a number of other explanations too. Lightning is caused by atoms rubbing together in clouds to produce fire. Or perhaps it's created when part of a cloud is tightly compressed. Epicurus was quite candid that he didn't know for sure and didn't have all the answers. Like a good scientist would do today, he simply put forward hypotheses that might plausibly make sense of what he'd observed. For instance, perhaps lightning reaches us before thunder does because lightning moves faster, he suggested. The speed of light is faster than the speed of sound. His attempts at explanations often referred to processes that people already understood from other contexts. Rubbing two sticks together can produce fire in the right conditions, so the fire-like lightning created in the clouds may also be the product of things rubbing together. Epicurus didn't know for sure, but he was highly confident that the truth lay in an explanation of this kind. That's certainly far more plausible than claiming that lightning comes from the thunderbolt of Zeus and that when it occurs it is a sign of divine displeasure. As Epicurus put it, 'it is possible that the thunderbolt may be caused in still other ways. Only let there be an end to mythologizing!'

The study of these sorts of natural phenomena, then, can help us to avoid coming up with fanciful accounts of how these things happen. Epicurus made explicit to his friend the purpose of all this:

> If you remember these various points, Pythocles, you will keep clear of religious superstition for the most part and be able to comprehend related matters.

All this makes it sound as if Epicurus was a deeply irreligious figure. Over the centuries the Epicureans have often been attacked as atheists, and many modern admirers are drawn to Epicureanism precisely because they see it as an atheistic philosophy. But Epicurus did not deny the existence of gods. What he did deny is that they play any active role in the day-to-day management of the universe. One of the key characteristics of a divine being, Epicurus claimed, is happiness, and that is simply incompatible with the stresses and strains of being responsible for running anything, let alone the entire cosmos. Equally, happiness cannot be reconciled with the traditional Greek view of the gods as vengeful, bickering figures.

So, what did Epicurus think the gods were like? They are happy and immortal. 'The gods do indeed exist,' he wrote, 'but they are not like what the masses suppose them to be.' As if pre-empting the sorts of criticisms one might expect such a view to attract, he continued:

> The irreligious man is not the person who destroys the gods of the masses but the person who imposes the ideas of the masses on the gods.

Those ideas of the masses all ultimately come down to assuming that the gods are basically like ordinary people, just more powerful. Thus they reward good behaviour and punish bad; they get angry, engage in deception, and have family quarrels. But none of that can be right, Epicurus claimed, because it goes against the state of calm tranquillity that he took to be a fundamental characteristic of a divine being.

What were these Epicurean gods like and where did they live? The Epicurean commitment to the idea that everything is composed of atoms suggests that the gods too are material beings composed of the same substance as everything else. Lucretius described them as having a 'flimsy nature' and being 'scarcely visible'. Their home is beyond the limits of our world, from which they are completely disconnected. We needn't offer thanks to them for creating the world, because they didn't. Just a passing acquaintance with geography, Lucretius commented, will show that the earth clearly wasn't created for our benefit, given that 'almost two-thirds are withheld from mankind by torrid heat and perennial deposits of frost'.

So the gods do exist, but they exist in their own flimsy world beyond the reach of ours. They didn't create our world, and they take no interest in it. Instead they live there in blessed tranquillity. Horace summed up the Epicurean view like this:

> I have learned that the gods live a life of calm, and that if nature performs a miracle, it's not sent down by the gods in anger from their high home in the sky.

All of this may sound fanciful to say the least, especially from someone who claimed to be giving a naturalistic account of the physical world. What's the evidence? Obviously Epicurus had no direct experience of these serene beings. But the principles of his physics gave him reason to believe that they must exist somewhere. For if the universe is infinite – that is, an infinite void containing an infinite number of atoms – then every conceivable combination of atoms will exist somewhere. There will be a vast variety of galaxies and solar systems and planets, each the product of some slightly different chance combination of atoms. One of these will be home to the Epicurean gods.

Whatever one thinks of all this, Epicurus's guiding principle throughout remained the goal of a calm and tranquil life. His gods have no interest in human affairs, and so we have no need to fear divine punishment in either this life or any other. But they also provide an image of tranquillity to which we might aspire. The highest beings that exist in the Epicurean universe enjoy a peaceful, untroubled life, and so might we.

Few people today worry about the vengeful thunderbolt of Zeus, so what lesson can we abstract from this? The central thought at work here is that many of our fears and concerns are based on partial and confused information about how the world works. By studying nature we can come to see that whatever happens is simply the product of a mundane physical process working itself out.

There are no tragedies or disasters or punishments; there's just dispassionate matter in motion, which in itself is nothing to fear. The only genuinely bad thing is pain, for which Epicurus has his other remedies.

06

Don't Fear
Death

WE DON'T KNOW precisely when or how, but we all know that at some point we shall die. This is in many ways the single most important fact there is. It defines us as mortal beings. It limits the amount of time we have, which adds a sense of urgency to our plans and projects. That we don't know when it will happen can also lead to a sense of anxiety. Then there's the question of what, if anything, comes next.

Philodemus's fourfold remedy says that we ought not to worry about death. Epicurus himself was even more to the point: 'death is nothing to us'. This became a central theme in Epicurean philosophy, suggesting that in antiquity there was a real anxiety about death that needed to be addressed. Epicurus discussed the topic in his *Letter to Menoeceus*, Lucretius added further arguments in his great poem, while Philodemus devoted an entire treatise to the subject, in four books.

Let's start with Epicurus. His core idea, as we've already seen, is that pleasure is the only good and pain the only bad thing. Both pleasure and pain are things that we experience via sensation. But what's death? It's the absence of sensation. Someone who is dead experiences nothing, by definition. If death is the absence of sensation, then it contains neither pleasure nor pain, and so is neither good nor bad. If it's neither good nor bad – if it's simply the absence of all sensation – then it's nothing worth fearing.

Part of the problem lies in our inability

to grasp the idea of our own non-existence.
Even that is an awkward way of putting it.
It won't be 'our' non-existence, because we
shall no longer exist. We shall never *be* dead,
because after our deaths we won't *be* at all.
Someone who asks the question 'What will
happen to me when I'm dead?' has failed to
grasp the fact that there is no 'I' after death.
That's it; death is the end of everything. If
there is some kind of post-mortem existence,
that just means the event we now call death
isn't really death at all, but merely a moment
of transformation in our ongoing existence
as conscious beings. But Epicurus had no
time for thoughts like that. He believed that
we are embodied human beings, made out
of physical atoms, and that when our bodies
die and their atoms are dispersed that's the
end of us. When that happens, there is no
'I' to experience anything, and experiencing
nothing is neither good nor bad because it
involves neither pleasure nor pain. But once
again we are caught in awkward language:

does it even make sense to say 'experiencing nothing' when there's no one there to do the experiencing?

According to Epicurus, grasping this key point will immediately make our lives more pleasant. He wrote:

> There is nothing fearful in living for the person who has really laid hold of the fact there is nothing fearful in not living.

His line of thought went like this. What do you really fear in life? Perhaps it's hunger, poverty, illness, violent assault. It's probably something that you think will harm you and, taken to extremes, may even kill you. In part it's a quite natural fear of physical pain but it's also, ultimately, a fear of death. But if death is nothing to be feared, for the reasons already given, then none of these things are worth fearing either. What's the worst thing that can happen to you when you are alive? That you die. But if that's no longer worth worrying about, then none of these other things ought to bother us either, or certainly not as much as they often do.

At this point a sceptic might say that our fear of these things – hunger, illness, assault, indeed death itself – is in large part due to the pain that accompanies them. Even if death understood as non-existence is nothing to be concerned about, we might be deeply concerned about the suffering that all too often accompanies the process of dying. Epicurus would of course acknowledge this; after all, for him pain is the only genuinely bad thing. So how would he respond to this kind of concern?

I think he'd respond in two ways. The first would be to say, as we saw earlier, that physical pain falls into two broad types: it is usually either mild or short-lived. Mild ongoing pain, although hardly desirable, can be coped with, and many of us do so without too much complaint. Intense pain, Epicurus claimed, is usually short-lived. If it's really intense and continues for a while, this probably indicates something that will kill us, bringing it to its own natural end. In either case, whatever pain we do suffer is usually offset by a variety of pleasures that we experience at the same time, even if we might often underestimate how many these are.

The second response would be to say that although physical pain is indeed bad, it is nowhere near as bad as psychological pain. The fear of death can far outweigh the pain associated with a terminal illness, he would suggest, and that is more likely to be true for us, now that we have all the benefits of modern palliative care. Similarly with hunger: people can easily cope with the pain of hunger for a short while, as attested by the experiences of those fasting or on diets, but the fear of being unable to feed oneself at all in times of need is far more difficult to ignore. Physical pain is relatively easy to cope with; it's psychological pain that is much harder to handle.

Epicurus's arguments that death ought

to be of no concern to us were repeated by
Lucretius. He too stressed that fear of death
is often produced by a failure really to grasp
that we'll no longer be around. We can only
suffer if we exist, and death is non-existence.
As he put it:

> One who no longer is cannot suffer, or differ in
> any way from one who has never been born.

Lucretius also noted that we are completely
indifferent to the fact that we did not exist
before we were born. Indeed, for the vast
majority of the history of the planet – let
alone the universe as a whole – we didn't
exist. That fact hardly keeps us awake at
night. Lucretius commented that if that's the
case, then we clearly don't have a problem
with our own non-existence as such. If non-
existence before birth is not a problem, then
why be concerned with non-existence after
our deaths?

One reason why we might be more concerned about our non-existence after death

is that it rids us of our present life and all
the opportunities that come with it. I didn't
miss out on anything by not being alive the
year before I was born, for if I had been born
a year earlier I would have been a different
person. But there are all sorts of things I
could potentially do the year after my death,
if only I had lived a bit longer. In other
words, even if I accepted Epicurus's argu-
ment that death ought to be of no concern,
I might still be very concerned about how
long my life turns out to be. I may not have
a problem with some abstract future state
of non-existence that I'll never be around to
experience, but I might still be very exercised
by the thought of dying next week rather
than in thirty or forty years' time. Just think
of all those extra decades full of further
pleasures waiting to be enjoyed.

This concern did not escape the attention of the ancient Epicureans. We find it
addressed in Philodemus's *On Death*, an
extended work in four books, of which we

have fragments recovered from the charred
papyri at Herculaneum. What matters
most, Philodemus argued, is the quality, not
quantity, of life. There are all sorts of cases
where a long life might be no blessing at all,
if, say, it is especially miserable. The belief
that a longer life is automatically better than
a shorter one is just too simplistic. In order
to come up with something more nuanced,
Philodemus drew on Epicurus's account of
different types of pleasure. The goal, you'll
recall, is to reach a state of static pleasure,
the contentment of not being hungry. That
kind of pleasure is complete and cannot be
improved by adding any more active pleasure to it. When someone has attained this
state of contentment, there is nothing that
can make it any better – things are as perfect
as they can be. Now, whether this state of
contentment lasts for five minutes or fifty
years doesn't make a significant difference,
for all we can ever enjoy is contentment in
the present moment. Because this is some-

thing qualitative, not quantitative, how long it lasts for doesn't add anything to the experience, in the sense that it doesn't make our experience in the present moment any better than it already is. If you can reach this kind of contentment in the here and now then your life is as complete as it can get, no matter how long it lasts. We can, Philodemus wrote, 'profit from one day as we would from eternity'. Or as Epicurus himself had put it, 'infinite time contains no greater pleasure than does finite time'. Rather than waste our mental energies worrying about what happens at death, how long our lives will be, or what we might miss out on, the Epicurean lesson is that we should focus on enjoying the life we have, which we can only live in the present moment. As Horace famously put it, we ought to 'seize the day' (*carpe diem*), and spend a bit less time worrying about tomorrow. But the final word ought to go to Epicurus himself and this powerful wake-up call:

We are born once. We cannot be born a second time, and throughout eternity we shall of necessity no longer exist. You have no power over tomorrow, and yet you put off your pleasure. Life is ruined by procrastination, and every one of us dies deep in his affairs.

07

Explaining
Everything

WE HAVE ALLUDED a couple of times to the fact that Epicurus was an atomist. Indeed, atomism was the foundation of his whole philosophy. It's an incredibly simple and elegant theory that claims to offer an explanation of literally everything – not just physical bodies but also minds, the mechanism of perception, the origin of order generated out of chaos, and the rise and fall of civilizations. All this is laid out in the magnificent poem by Lucretius, *On the Nature of Things*. As we have already seen, we know very little about

Lucretius himself, except that he lived in the first century BC and may have been part of a wider community of Epicureans in the Bay of Naples area, including Philodemus and perhaps Virgil.

His poem survived the Middle Ages in just a handful of copies. Largely neglected during those centuries, it was brought back out of the shadows in the fifteenth century when Papal secretary turned book hunter Poggio Bracciolini uncovered a copy in a monastery in southern Germany. He quickly dispatched it to a friend in Florence, who had copies made that circulated and contributed to the burgeoning interest in Epicureanism during the Renaissance. Alas, the manuscript found by Poggio has since been lost, but two other early copies survive, both dating back to the ninth century, which now reside in the university library at Leiden.

It is in many ways quite an odd work – a poem addressed to a goddess that goes on to offer a completely naturalistic account of,

well, everything. Since the recovery of parts
of Epicurus's *On Nature* from the papyri
at Herculaneum, scholars have shown that
Lucretius was following Epicurus's text
closely, producing a faithful account of his
ideas, transformed into Latin verse. Lucretius gives us a full account of Epicurean
atomism, which was based on the earlier
atomism of the Greek philosopher Democri-
tus. The basic idea is that everything that
exists is composed of atoms – the building
blocks of nature – that move around in an
infinite void. Lucretius puts it like this:

> So many atoms, clashing together in so many
> ways as they are swept along through infinite
> time by their own weight, have come together
> in every possible way and realized everything
> that could be formed by their combinations.

The atoms themselves were thought to
be indestructible (*atomos* literally means
'uncuttable'), neither created nor destroyed.
They come in a variety of shapes, helping

to explain the variety of physical elements within nature. They also have weight, but not colour, taste, or smell, which are the product of interactions between atoms coming off objects and our sense organs.

Lucretius had no hesitation in explaining every aspect of human life in terms of atomic interactions. We have already seen him insist that death, understood as the destruction of our current atomic arrangement, is the end of us. Our mental life and our sensations can also be explained simply in terms of atomic movements, just as materialist philosophers still try to do today. Different tastes and smells, for instance, can be explained by differing textures of the variously shaped atoms. 'When something sweet to one is bitter to another,' Lucretius commented, 'it must be because its smoothest particles palpably penetrate the palate of the former, whereas the latter's gullet is evidently invaded by particles that are rough and jagged.' This can also explain why some plants can be poisonous to humans but not to some other animals, and why things can smell differently when one is ill. Although Lucretius inevitably didn't have all the details worked out, he was clear that atomism could one day offer a comprehensive account of all aspects of our existence.

To get a sense of Lucretius's intellectual ambitions, it is worth focusing on the history of the universe that he gives, from the formation of the cosmos, through the origins of life on earth, to the rise and fall of human civilizations. The persistent theme throughout his account is that everything, no matter how large or small, is subject to creation and destruction. Although the atoms themselves were thought to be indestructible, everything made from them is mutable and will at some point break apart. Even the earth and the sky, Lucretius comments, came into being at a certain point in time and will eventually be destroyed. Everything is in a state of perpetual flux, the product of unending atomic motion. Even the sun, worshipped by some as a god, is slowly dissipating with each radiance of light, 'for ever losing flash after flash of flame, not an enduring essence untouched by time'.

If everything is mutable and will ultimately be destroyed, equally everything had to be created at some point. Lucretius suggested that our world is a relatively recent creation. It was formed out of chance and unplanned collisions of atoms, during which earth and air separated out due to their differing weights into planet and atmosphere. Lucretius attempts to describe how this might have happened:

> Day by day the encircling ethereal fires and the sun's rays by continual bombardment of the outer crust from every quarter compressed the earth into an ever narrower compass, so that it shrank into itself in its middle reaches and cohered more compactly.

While all this is inevitably speculation, the modernity of Lucretius's account can be unsettling at times. But he is also all too aware of the limits of his knowledge, at one point outlining a series of plausible explanations for celestial movements and eclipses, simply concluding that which of them is most likely to be true 'lies beyond the range of our stumbling progress'. Sometimes he was inevitably wildly off the mark, such as when claiming that the sun is only as large as it appears to us, but current theories about the generation and destruction of stars and planets were in a crude form pre-empted by our Epicurean poet some two thousand years ago. If Lucretius's poem was indeed based on Epicurus's *On Nature*, then credit should go further back to Epicurus himself.

After the formation of the planet came the development of life on earth, starting with vegetation, then the appearance of animals. In those early days in the earth's history, Lucretius comments that 'many species must have died out altogether'. Those that survived did so 'either by cunning or by prowess or by speed'. Those without such benefits 'were fair game and an easy prey for others'. In short, what he was describing is survival of the fittest. The chance and contingent nature of the development of animal species is of course merely an echo of the random atomic movements underlying these larger-scale processes.

Among the prehistoric animals were early humans, much tougher than those of today, living nomadic lives like wild beasts. They did not yet know how to make use of fire. Lucretius goes on to describe the origins of human civilization: humans began to build huts, clothe themselves in skins, harness fire, form family units, and so on. They developed mutual alliances for the sake of protection. If they hadn't done all this:

> . . . the entire human race would have been wiped out there and then, instead of being propagated, generation after generation, down to the present day.

Next came the development of language, followed by cities, private property, and the rule of law. In an attempt to understand the world in which they lived, in particular celestial phenomena, people created images of divine beings, and organized religion soon followed.

An important moment in human history was the discovery of copper and iron. Lucretius gives some highly speculative attempts to explain how primitive humans first harnessed the power of fire for smelting metal. The important point, though, is that there's no myth in which Prometheus had to steal fire from the gods. It can all be accounted for naturalistically. Human arts developed gradually over time; early humans groped their way forward through trial, error, and experience. The fine arts did not require divine inspiration either: birdsong inspired singing, while the wind blowing through reeds inspired the creation of the first musical instruments.

One lesson that Lucretius takes from his attempt to sketch the history of human development is the contingency and arbitrariness of the trappings of his own time:

> . . . skins yesterday, purple and gold today – such are the baubles that embitter human life with resentment and waste it with war.

The primitive desire for skins in order to keep warm was, in Epicurus's terms, entirely natural and necessary. The problem is that we transfer that desire to the 'purple and gold' togas of Roman generals, consuls and, later, the Emperor, thinking that these too are essential, when in fact they're unnecessary. As a consequence of this mistake:

> . . . mankind is perpetually the victim of a pointless and futile martyrdom, fretting life away in fruitless worries through failure to realize what limit is set to acquisition and to the growth of genuine pleasure.

As we can see, practical lessons are never far

away from Lucretius's account of the origin and development of human civilization. It effectively serves multiple Epicurean ends at once. It removes supernatural explanations from the picture – such things are simply not required. It also highlights where the trappings of modern civilization ultimately came from, in the process stressing their contingency. In so doing, it reminds us of which things were developed to serve real human needs, and which are merely unnecessary embellishments. Lest his readers forget, Lucretius regularly inserts reminders that this poem combining cosmology and anthropology is fundamentally offering lessons in how to live:

> If a man would guide his life by true philosophy, he will find ample riches in a modest livelihood enjoyed with a tranquil mind.

This brings us back to the core ideas of Epicureanism: a simple life and peace of mind. The lesson to take away from Lucretius is that in order to attain these things we need to understand the way the world works from a dispassionate, scientific perspective. Only then can we know what we really need in order to live well and how to escape the irrational fears that all too often disturb us.

Epilogue

EPICURUS, LIKE EVERYONE else, eventually had to face his own death. Ancient sources report that the final stages of his life were marked by illness and intense pain. For someone who saw pain as a genuinely bad thing, this was surely a rough process to have to go through. No otherworldly consolation or high-minded morality was available to him; just the reality of intense physical pain. Yet the ancient reports that we have paint a picture of someone serene in the face of physical suffering, not to mention his own

imminent end. We have seen already that
death itself would have been of no concern to
him, but the pain of dying was another matter. How did he cope with this? As it happens, we have an account from Epicurus
himself, a short letter to his friend and follower Idomeneus, in which he says:

> On this blissful day, which is also the last
> of my life, I write this to you. My continual
> sufferings from strangury and dysentery are so
> great that nothing could augment them; but
> over against them all I set gladness of mind at
> the remembrance of our past conversations.

The happy memories of past pleasures with
a good friend were enough to see Epicurus
through the physical discomfort of his illness
in its final hours. His companions who
witnessed how he coped during his last days
were evidently impressed, given the tributes
that they paid to him after his death. The
commemoration of Epicurus's birthday and
the erection of statues in his image suggest

that the early Epicureans admired the man himself as much as they did his teachings. Although Epicureanism dropped out of sight for much of the Middle Ages, the fifteenth century saw the rediscovery of both Epicurus's letters and sayings, recorded by Diogenes Laertius, and Lucretius's *On the Nature of Things*. Manuscripts of Diogenes Laertius were brought to Italy from Byzantium and translated into Latin by the monk Ambrogio Traversari. Since then, Epicurean philosophy has found regular admirers, especially during the scientific revolution of the seventeenth century, which built on Epicurean atomism. Despite its ongoing reputation for sensualism and atheism, the Catholic priest Pierre Gassendi championed Epicureanism, revising its atomism and hedonism in order to make it acceptable to an early modern Christian audience. It found a quite different admirer in the young Karl Marx, who wrote his university dissertation on Epicurean philosophy. Marx admired the

rationalism and materialism of Epicurus,
as well as the polemics against superstition,
writing:

> Philosophy, as long as a drop of blood shall
> pulse in its world-subduing and absolutely
> free heart, will never grow tired of answering
> its adversaries with the cry of Epicurus.

More recently people have been drawn to
Epicureanism for a variety of reasons, not
least the way in which it seamlessly fits
with our modern scientific world view. But
regardless of how much or how little of
Epicurean philosophy one might agree with,
many of the issues that the ancient Epicureans discussed are as relevant today as when
they were first raised in a private garden on
the edge of ancient Athens.

Further Reading

EPICURUS'S THREE LETTERS, his collection of *Key Doctrines*, and an ancient biography of him can all be found in Book 10 of Diogenes Laertius's *Lives of the Philosophers*. Much of this, along with some of the *Vatican Sayings*, is translated in Epicurus, *The Art of Happiness*, trans. G. K. Strodach (Penguin, 2012). Another collection worth noting is *The Epicurus Reader*, ed. Brad Inwood and L. P. Gerson (Hackett, 1994).

Lucretius's great poem has been translated multiple times. There is an older Penguin translation into prose by R. E. Latham (quoted in this book), first published in 1951, and a more recent translation into rhyming couplets: Lucretius, *On the Nature of Things*, trans. A. E. Stallings (Penguin, 2007). The story of its rediscovery during the Renaissance is told in S. Greenblatt, *The Swerve: How the Renaissance Began* (The Bodley Head, 2011).

A number of works by Philodemus are now available in English, including Philodemus, *On Death*, trans. W. B. Henry (Society of Biblical Literature, 2009). For an excellent illustrated account of the Herculaneum papyri, see D. Sider, *The Library of the Villa dei Papiri at Herculaneum* (Getty Publications, 2005).

Horace's *Satires* can be found alongside his *Epistles* and the *Satires* of Persius, trans. N. Rudd (Penguin, 1979). On Epicurean themes in Horace, see S. Yona, *Epicurean Ethics in Horace* (Oxford University Press, 2018).

The inscription erected by Diogenes of Oenoanda is reconstructed and translated in M. F. Smith's *Diogenes of Oinoanda: The Epicurean Inscription* (Bibliopolis, 1993).

For fuller accounts of Epicurean philosophy see T. O'Keefe, *Epicureanism* (Acumen/ University of California Press, 2010), C. Wilson, *Epicureanism: A Very Short Introduction* (Oxford University Press, 2015), and, considered within the wider philosophical context of the period, my own *Hellenistic Philosophy* (Oxford University Press, 2018).

Therapeutic aspects of Epicureanism are discussed in M. Nussbaum's *The Therapy of Desire: Theory and Practice in Hellenistic Ethics* (Princeton University Press, 1994) and in V. Tsouna's essay 'Epicurean Therapeutic Strategies', in J. Warren, ed., *The Cambridge Companion to Epicureanism* (Cambridge University Press, 2009). For an account of how people might learn from Epicureanism today, see C. Wilson, *How to Be an Epicurean* (Basic Books, 2019).

References

PROLOGUE Goethe refers to half-Stoic and half-Epicurean people in *Characteristics of Goethe* (London, 1833), vol. 1, p. 99. Albert Ellis mentions Epicurus in many places, including his book (co-authored with Robert Harper) *A Guide to Rational Living* (Chatsworth, CA: Wilshire, 1997), p. 5.

CHAPTER 1 'Empty are the words . . .' is recorded in Porphyry's *To Marcella* 31. Details about Epicurus's life come from the biography in Diogenes Laertius 10.1–

29. Pliny the Elder mentions the practices of Roman Epicureans in *Natural History* 35.2.5. The passages from Diogenes Oenoanda both come from fr. 3 in M. F. Smith's *Diogenes of Oinoanda: The Epicurean Inscription* (Naples: Bibliopolis, 1993). 'No one should postpone . . .' and the subsequent quotation are from *Ep. Men.* 122. Albert Ellis mentions Epicureanism, Stoicism, and Buddhism together in Windy Dryden, ed., *Rational Emotive Behaviour Therapy: A Reader* (London: Sage, 1995), pp. 1–2. For Memmius and the ruins of Epicurus's house, see Cicero's letter to Memmius in his *Letters to Friends* (*Fam.* 13.1). 'This dread and darkness . . .' is from Lucretius 1.146–8 (and is repeated at 2.59–61, 3.91–3, 6.39–41). Virgil's 'Happy is he . . .' is from his *Georgics* 2.490–2.

CHAPTER 2 Horace's remark 'fat and flourishing . . .' comes from his *Letters* (*Ep.* 1.4). Ancient criticisms of Epicurus are reported in Diogenes Laertius 10.6–7. Epicurus's 'bodily pleasure . . .' is *Key Doctrine* 18, while 'No pleasure is bad . . .' is *Key Doctrine* 8. Horace's 'the highest pleasure . . .' is from *Satire* 2.2.19–20. 'On the contrary . . .' is from *Ep. Men.* 132; 'Think about these . . .' is from *Ep. Men.* 135.

CHAPTER 3 Epicurus's reflections on different types of desire are in *Ep. Men.* 127–8. Horace's 'Nothing is enough . . .' is from *Satires* 1.1.61–3; 'Maybe you prefer . . .' is from 1.1.76–8. 'Nature's wealth . . .' is *Key Doctrine* 15; 'One who understands . . .' is *Key Doctrine* 21. Epicurus's 'nothing is sufficient . . .' is *Vatican Saying* 68. His reference to bread and water is reported in Diogenes Laertius 10.11, while 'understand better . . .' is from *Vatican Saying* 44. 'A free person . . .' is *Vatican Saying* 67.

CHAPTER 4 Epicurus's reflections on friendship are preserved in the *Vatican Sayings*.

The remark about help and confidence is in *Vatican Saying* 34; the risk of commercial transaction is in *Vatican Saying* 39. Horace's reflections on friendship are in *Satire* 1.3; 'My kind friends . . .' is at 1.3.139–41. 'Friendship dances . . .' is *Vatican Saying* 52.

CHAPTER 5 Epicurus wrote 'if a person . . .' in *Ep. Pyth.* 96 and 'it is possible . . .' in *Ep. Pyth.* 104. 'If you remember . . .' is from *Ep. Pyth.* 116. 'The gods do indeed exist . . .' is from *Ep. Men.* 123, as is 'The irreligious man . . .'. Lucretius's remarks about the gods are at 5.146–55; 'almost two-thirds . . .' is from 5.204–5. Horace's 'I have learned . . .' is *Satire* 1.5.101–3.

CHAPTER 6 Epicurus's reflections on death are in his *Letter to Menoeceus* 124–7; 'There is nothing fearful . . .' is from *Ep. Men.* 125. Lucretius's 'One who no longer is . . .' is at 3.867–8. Philodemus wrote 'profit from one day' in *On Death* 38.18–19. Epicurus's 'infinite time . . .' is *Key Doctrine* 19. Horace's 'seize the day' is from *Odes* 1.11. Epicurus's 'We are born once . . .' is *Vatican Saying* 14.

CHAPTER 7 Most of the passages from Lucretius in this chapter come from Book 5 of *On the Nature of Things*. 'So many atoms . . .' is from 5.187–90. 'When something sweet . . .' is from 4.658–62. The destruction of earth and sky is mentioned at 5.245–6, while 'for ever losing flash . . .' is at 5.304–5 (slightly modified here). 'Day by day . . .' is from 5.483–6 and 'lies beyond . . .' is from 5.532–3. The passages discussing 'many species' and 'easy prey' are in 5.855–77; 'the entire human race . . .' is from 5.1026–7; 'skins yesterday . . .' is from 5.1423–4; 'mankind is perpetually . . .' is from 5.1430–2; 'If a man would guide . . .' is from 5.1117–19.

EPILOGUE Epicurus's letter to Idomeneus can be found in Diogenes Laertius 10.22. For further discussion of the later reception of Epicureanism, see H. Jones, *The Epicurean Tradition* (London: Routledge, 1989), and C. Wilson, *Epicureanism at the Origins of Modernity* (Oxford: Clarendon Press, 2008). Marx's dissertation can be found in Volume 1 of K. Marx and F. Engels, *Collected Works* (London: Lawrence & Wishart, 1975); the quotation is from p. 30.